English Skills

3

Skills

for Primary Students
3rd Edition

Grammar & Punctuation

John Barwick
Jenny Barwick

Five Senses Education Pty Ltd
2/195 Prospect Highway
Seven Hills 2147
New South Wales
Australia

Copyright © John Barwick and Jenny Barwick
First Published by Horwitz Education 2002.
Second edition published by Oxford University Press 2007.
Third edition published by Five Senses Education 2021.

Barwick, John & Barwick, Jenny
English skills for primary students 3: grammar and punctuation
3rd edition
ISBN 978-1-76032-374-5

Introduction

The *English Skills for Primary Students* series has been designed to promote and support the development of a high standard of English language use—an essential asset for academic success, and success in the world beyond school.

This series comprises four graded books focusing on the development of skills needed for success at primary school.

English Skills for Primary Students 3: Grammar and Punctuation covers the skills appropriate for Year 3 students. Topics include parts of speech, phrases and clauses, and punctuation. An easy to follow answer section is located at the back of the book. Although designed for use at home, the *English Skills for Primary Students* series also provides teachers with a comprehensive English classroom program.

There are four Reviews included in this edition of English Skills for Primary Students. The Review Answers are available online at *http://www.fivesenseseducation.com.au/english-skills-p3-9781760323745*. These Review Answers are PDF documents that you can print and save to your computer for future use.

Language is central to all of our lives. A child who can understand and use English well is more likely to experience success in all subjects studied at school. This book will improve your child's skills in English by explicitly demonstrating how the English language works.

Contents

Unit 1

Nouns

A **noun** is a word that names a person, place or thing.

1 Circle the noun in each of the pairs of words below. The first one is done for you.

(hat) / in	up / book	beach / the
cow / ran	girl / a	huge / Jupiter
face / cleaned	my / uncle	game / played
sky / under	triangle / has	often / brother
Peter / to	hamburger / cooked	swam / Sydney

2 Match the nouns to the people, places and things they name.

desk	teacher	mirror	apple	backpack	shirt
	bottle	window			

a A bag worn on the back is called a ....

b An .... is a type of fruit.

c An opening in the wall of a building is called a ....

d A .... is something in which you can see yourself.

e A person who instructs a class is called a ....

f A .... is an item of clothing.

g A glass container is called a ....

h A special table for writing or working on a computer is often called a ....

Find the nouns in each sentence and underline them. There may be more than one noun.

a The woman was very old.

b We bought a new table and four chairs.

c The teacher smiled at the class.

d My canary sings beautifully.

e Our new car doesn't fit into the garage.

f There were twenty books on the shelf.

g The house next to ours burnt down last night.

h The cyclone swept through the town, damaging many buildings.

Use the clues to unjumble the nouns in brackets. Write your answer on the line.

a a place to have a swim   (loop) ....

b a thing you can write on   (preap) ....

c something which burns in a fire   (olg) ....

d what you use to tidy your hair   (hursb) ....

e a large vehicle which can carry heavy loads   (kruct) ....

f a winter month in Australia   (luyJ) ....

g a musical instrument with white and
black keys   (anipo) ....

h an orange root vegetable   (tarcor) ....

Unit 2  Common nouns

Common nouns are the names of ordinary things you can hear, see, smell, touch or taste.

Examples: sister   television   fire   grape   fence   sea

Checkpoint!   Common nouns only begin with a capital letter when they are the first word in a sentence.

Examples: Trees were uprooted during the storm.
We sat under the shady trees.

 1   **Circle the common noun in each of the pairs of words below. The first one is done for you.**

city / Canberra   raced / bus   Australia / country

diver / dived   planet / Neptune   tiny / mouse

Murray / river   ocean / Pacific   soccer / kicked

boy / Matthew   June / month   calmly / aeroplane

cake / delicious   Christmas / holiday Victoria / state

 2   **Fill the gaps in the sentences with the correct noun.**

| kitchen   pea   supermarket   platypus   disk |
| light   wheels   ocean |

a   A .... is a native Australian animal that lives in creeks and rivers.

b   A .... is a room where meals are prepared.

c   Cars travel on discs called ....

d   We turn on a .... when it gets dark.

e A .... is a small, round, green vegetable.

f Another word for the sea is ....

g Information can be stored on a computer ....

h The place where you can buy many food items is a ....

Find the common nouns in each sentence and underline them. There is more than one common noun in each sentence.

a Our school has six hundred pupils.

b My brother plays soccer.

c The rain fell so heavily that the creek flooded.

d Our neighbour has just bought a new car.

e Our teacher likes ice-cream.

f Be careful not to upset the can of worms.

g The kangaroo bounded across the treeless plain.

h During winter, snow falls on the mountains.

Use the clues to help you unjumble the names of Australian animals. Write your answers on the line.

a a sea cow   (dungog) ....

b a burrowing animal   (twambo) ....

c Australian "Easter Bunny"   (blyib) ....

d a monotreme with quills   (chednia) ....

e not a real bear   (aloka) ....

f looks like a tiny kangaroo   (oporoto) ....

g lives in trees and roofs   (spomus) ....

h a carnivorous reptile   (olcrodice) ....

Unit 3 — Proper nouns

Proper nouns are the names of particular people, places or things.

Examples: Melbourne Shark Bay Saturn Subaru January Jessica

Checkpoint! Proper nouns begin with a capital letter.

1 Circle the proper noun in each of the pairs of words below. The first one is done for you.

Tasmania / state   Tokyo / city   France / country

Theo / nephew   Thursday / day   holiday / Easter

mountain / Mt Warning lake / Torrens   Sally / cousin

sea / Mediterranean   month / October   Emerald / town

Murrumbidgee / river   Kakadu / reserve   governor / Phillip

2 Find the proper nouns in each sentence and underline them.

a Last night the plane from Darwin was thirty minutes late.

b Michelle and Sarah wrote their recount of the excursion together.

c Our mower is a Victa.

d Canberra is the capital city of Australia.

e We always cross Lang Road at the pedestrian crossing.

f When I was younger, my favourite book was *Blinky Bill*.

g Bass Strait separates Tasmania from Victoria.

h Many tourists visit Alice Springs.

Use the proper nouns to fill the gaps in the sentences below.

Parkes   September   India   Hume Highway
Pacific Ocean   Corolla   Canberra   Friday

a My birthday is in ....

b There is a famous radio telescope near
    the town of ....

c We stopped at .... on our way
    to Sydney.

d Our car is a Toyota ....

e .... is a nation in Asia.

f The largest ocean in the world is
    the ....

g The .... joins
    Sydney and Melbourne.

h The school assembly is held every ....

**Write your own proper nouns to match the common nouns.
Use different nouns to those in Exercise 1.**

teacher	....	town	....
holiday	....	month	....
friend	....	car	....
street	....	park	....
day	....	city	....
country	....	ocean	....
school	....	state	....

Collective Nouns

> A **collective noun** is the name of a group of people or things. For example, the word **crowd** is a collective noun we use to name a group of people.

 1 **Match the nouns to the groups of people in the sentences.**

class	choir	gang	team	crew	band

a A group of people who work on a ship is called its ....

b A group of people who play instruments and sing together is called a ....

c A group of people who sing together is called a ....

d A group of people who play sport together is called a ....

e A group of students with the same teacher is called a ....

f A group of convicts was called a ....

 2 **Fill the gaps in the following sentences with the correct collective noun.**

swarm	batch	herd	bunch	school	mob

a I gave my teacher a .... of flowers.

b The beekeeper was not stung, even though she was surrounded by a .... of bees.

c The .... of fish swam close to the boat.

d A .... of kangaroos bounded away from the billabong.

e The class ran into the classroom like a .... of elephants.

f The second .... of scones was better than the first.

Circle the correct collective noun in the sentences below.

a We bought a (hand / string) of bananas to take to the picnic.

b My grandfather takes a (pack / clump) of cards on long train trips.

c A (pod / swarm) of whales was seen in the bay yesterday.

d There were six puppies in the (gang / litter).

e We had to climb a long (cluster / flight) of stairs to reach the entrance.

f I collected some flowers for a (deck / posy) for my grandmother.

Draw lines to match the collective nouns with the groups of people or things they name.

squad	a group of seagulls
clutch	a line of vehicles travelling together
audience	a group of chickens
convoy	a group of wolves
pack	a large group of stars
gaggle	a group of soldiers
galaxy	a group of geese
regiment	a group of people watching a show
flock	a group of athletes on tour together

Unit 5

Singular and plural nouns

A **singular noun** means just one of something. The noun **book** is singular. It means just one book. A **plural noun** means more than one. The noun **books** is plural. It means more than one book.

1 **Circle the singular noun in each of the pairs of words below. The first one is done for you.**

(monkey) / monkeys   cliffs / cliff   babies / baby

octopus / octopuses   glasses / glass   women / woman

crops / crop   wave / waves   drum / drums

peaches / peach   bush / bushes   taxis / taxi

2 **Circle the plural noun in each of the pairs of words below. The first one is done for you.**

(cities) / city   tape / tapes   countries / country

dish / dishes   drain / drains   bus / buses

circuses / circus   packages / package   goose / geese

trolleys / trolley   month / months   rectangle / rectangles

We form the plural of many nouns simply by adding **s**.
If a word ends in **ch**, **sh**, **s** or **x**, then add **es**.

Example: one beach, two beaches.

3 **Write the plural of each singular noun below. The first one is done for you.**

shark   *sharks*   class   ....   kangaroo ....

bike   ....   fence   ....   sandwich ....

bucket ....   insect ....   dish   ....

answer ....   piece   ....   box   ....

thumb   ....   wish   ....   surprise ....

Write the singular form of each plural noun below. The first one is done for you.

sisters	*sister*	mice	....	brushes	....
poems	....	bananas	....	dresses	....
races	....	handles	....	patches	....
children	....	teeth	....	foxes	....
taxis	....	squares	....	houses	....

When a word ends in a vowel followed by a **y**, just add **s** to form the plural.

Example: valley / valleys

When a word ends in a consonant followed by a **y**, change the **y** to **i** and then add **es** to form the plural.

Example: sandfly / sandflies

 Write the plural of each singular noun on the lines. The first one is done for you.

jelly	*jellies*	way	....
birthday	....	body	....
family	....	party	....
donkey	....	holiday	....
lolly	....	berry	....

Write the singular of each plural noun on the lines.

keys	*key*	bodies	....
monkeys	....	ponies	....
ferries	....	fairies	....
boys	....	puppies	....

Articles

The words **a**, **an** and **the** are called **articles**. They are used in front of nouns. For example: **a** hat, **an** ambulance, **the** trees.

A and **an** are **indefinite articles**. We use them when we mean any one of a group, rather than a particular one. For example: May I have **a** donut, please?

We use **a** when the word which follows begins with a consonant. For example: **a b**ook or **a b**rown egg. We use **an** when the following word begins with a vowel. For example: **an o**range or **an a**ngry bee.

1 **Circle the correct article in each sentence.**

a (A / An) ambulance was called to the accident.

b (A / An) salad sandwich is a healthy lunch.

c May I borrow (a / an) pencil, please?

d We drove to the shops in (a / an) orange van.

e (A / An) ocean is a very large body of water.

f (A / An) pilot is someone who flies an aeroplane.

g Remember to bring (a / an) towel and your swimmers to the excursion.

h (A / An) helicopter landed on the football field.

i Mum has (a / an) old pair of joggers that she wears in the garden.

j My grandfather has (a / an) ancient watch.

The is the only **definite article**. We use it to refer to a particular person, place or thing. For example: May I have **the** ball, please?

Circle the most suitable article in each sentence.

a I would prefer a supreme pizza to (a / an / **the**) ham-and-pineapple pizza.

b The tiny boat drifted helplessly on (a / an / **the**) stormy waters of the lake.

c The fog lifted just as (a / an / **the**) sun set.

d A high area of land is called (**a** / an / the) hill.

e When I won the race I was (a / an / **the**) happiest person in the world.

f I took the money box to (a / an / **the**) office this morning.

There is a mistake in each sentence with a, an and the. Circle the mistake and write the most suitable article on the line. The first one is done for you.

a My father is (a) fastest runner in my family. ....*the*.......

b We had to leave a train at the last station. ....

c A capital city of South Australia is the city of Adelaide. ....

No wonder I am the fastest runner in the family!

d The sand dunes of the Simpson Desert are the bright red colour. ....

e Sarah tried out her new skateboard in an park just behind her house. ....

f A egg is a healthy way to start the day. ....

g My soccer team won because a goalie was able to save all the other team's shots. ....

h I went to the kitchen and got an apple from a fridge. ....

i The quickest way to get to the shops is by taking an short cut across the football field. ....

j I walked mud all over a new carpet. ....

Unit 7 Personal pronouns

Pronouns are words that can take the place of nouns.
I, you, she, he, it, we, you and they are pronouns that stand in the place of nouns doing the action in a sentence.

Example: Melissa has her own horse.
She has her own horse.

Checkpoint!   I, you, she, he, it, we, you and they are called personal pronouns.

1 Rewrite each of the sentences using she, he, it or they to stand for the noun groups in bold. The first one is done for you.

a **Tom** plays soccer.   *He plays soccer.*

b **Adesh** and **Caleb** are nine.   ....

c **Mrs Logan** read the book aloud. ....

d **My cousins** live in Canada.   ....

e **Oliver** came to my party   ....

f **The truck** was loaded with fruit.

....

g **The books** were stacked on the floor.
....

h **The snake** disappeared down a hole.
....

2 Fill the gaps in each sentence with I, you or we.

a I take my bodyboard when .... go to the beach with my family.

b You can read a book when .... have finished your work.

c When Brodie and I went to the zoo .... saw the seals being fed.

Circle the correct pronoun to replace the words in bold type in each sentence.

a	**My grandmother** rides a motorbike.	He It She
b	**The television** isn't working.	You They It
c	**Villa, Jacki and I** have been picked for the team.	They We You
d	**Ben** brought his own game.	He It She
e	**The pencil** is broken.	You They It
f	**The races** were over by lunchtime.	They It She
g	**Jessica** is in my class.	You They She
h	**The jellies** are nearly ready.	You They It

Choose the best pronoun below to fill the gaps in the sentences.

you   I   we   they   he   she

a My sister is late because .... missed the bus.

b When my family goes on holiday .... leave our dog at a boarding kennel.

c When you look through this window .... can see the ocean.

d I don't see my uncle very often because .... lives overseas.

e The shoes are wet because .... were left in the rain.

f I don't like carrots much but .... do like broccoli.

Review 1

1 Nouns

Circle the noun in each of the pairs of words below.

honey / on   by / computer   Melbourne / a

dog / jumped   sister / an   tiny / tree

egg / boiled   your / lunch   seat / broken

2 Common nouns

Find the common nouns in each sentence and underline them. Careful! One sentence has more than one common noun.

a Our class is small.

b My sister swims very well.

c The beach is very crowded.

d The stairs are slippery because of the rain.

3 Proper nouns

Underline the proper nouns in each sentence.

a Have you been to Adelaide?

b My cousins from overseas haven't eaten Vegemite.

c Have you read Double Helix?

d The Great Barrier Reef is off the coast of Queensland.

4 Collective nouns

Draw lines to match the collective nouns with the groups of people or things they name.

choir   a group of convicts

gang   a group of bees

crew   a group of elephants

herd   a group of singers

swarm   a group of people who work on a ship

5 Nouns can be singular or plural

Circle the plural noun in each of the pairs of words below.

beach / beaches   tape / tapes   months / month

surprise / surprises   ferries / ferry   holiday / holidays

child / children   geese / goose   taxi / taxis

Articles

Circle the best article to complete each sentence.

a   I would like a banana rather than (a / **an**) apple.

b   Grandpa has (a / **an** / the) old hat he loves to wear.

c   (A / An / **The**) computer is not connected. That's why you can't turn it on!

d   If you hurry you will catch (a / an / **the**) bus.

Personal pronouns

Circle the correct pronoun to replace the words in bold type in each sentence.

a   **The drinks** are in the fridge.   We   They   It

b   **My grandfather** loves working in his garden.   He   They   It

c   **The tent** is leaking.   He   It   She

d   **Jess, Max and I** are going to the game tomorrow.   They   It   We

Challenge

Find an example of each of the following in the passage below. Colour each a different colour and underline the plural nouns.

- common noun
- proper noun
- collective noun
- personal pronoun

My grandfather lives in Canberra. He loves to garden. When he is gardening he always wears his favourite hat. He likes it better than all his other hats. It stops him from getting sunburnt. It has other uses too. One day he used it to scare a flock of birds that were eating some seeds he had planted. He looked very funny running around the garden waving his old hat.

REVIEW 1 SELF-ASSESSMENT	Rate your progress		
	Needs work	Good effort	Fantastic
Common, proper and collective nouns	☆	☆☆	☆☆☆
Singular and plural nouns	☆	☆☆	☆☆☆
Articles	☆	☆☆	☆☆☆
Personal pronouns	☆	☆☆	☆☆☆
Highlight questions you would like to revise			

Me, you, her, him, it, us, you and them are pronouns that stand in the place of nouns **receiving** the action in a sentence. They usually follow the doing word (verb) in a sentence.

Example: Mrs Black drew the pictures.

Mrs Black drew **them**.

Checkpoint!   Me, you, her, him, it, us and them
are called **personal pronouns**.

1 Rewrite each of the sentences using her, him, it or them to stand for the nouns in bold type. The first one is done for you.

a I couldn't see **Tim and Paul**.   _I couldn't see them._

b Anna wrote **Sally** a letter.   ....

c Jacob put **the photo** in the folder.   ....

d I gave **my father** a golf ball.   ....

e We packed **the bags** quickly.   ....

f David told **Paul** the answer.   ....

g We visited **my aunt**.   ....

h I left **the towel** at the pool.   ....

2 Fill the gaps in each sentence with me, you or us.

a My brother gave .... a T-shirt for my birthday.

b Tom took ages to find .... when we hid behind the shed.

c After you tidy your room I will take .... to the beach.

Circle the correct pronoun to replace the words in bold in each sentence.

a Tom saw **Megan, Jacob and I** at the
bus stop.   them   us   we

b Simon lent **Stephanie** his racquet.   him   she   her

c We took **Ben** home.   him   it   he

d We cooked **the damper** in the fire.   you   they   it

e Luke picked **Brendan and Alex** for
his group.   they   him   them

f Put **the computer** on that desk.   you   them   it

g I rang **Nadine** last night.   she   them   her

h A large crowd watched **the boat** sink.   you   it   them

Choose the best pronoun below to fill the gaps in the sentences.

you	me	them	us	him	her

a Jessica's mother took .... to the doctor.

b My brother and I waited near the gate where Harry and Jack had said
they would meet ....

c "Jackie, take care or the beam will knock .... on
the head," called the captain to Jackie.

d My father's best friend beats .... every time
they play golf.

e The dogs barked because the thunder
frightened ....

f I hope my parents give .... a bike when
I turn eleven.

Unit 9 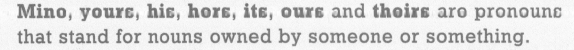 Possessive pronouns and pronoun check-up

Mine, yours, his, hers, its, ours and **theirs** are pronouns that stand for nouns owned by someone or something.

Example: The book on the table is **my book**.

The book on the table is **mine**.

Checkpoint! | **Mine, yours, his, hers, its, ours** and **theirs** are called **possessive pronouns**.

 1 **Underline the possessive pronouns in these sentences.**

a My ruler is broken. May I please borrow yours?

b That car is theirs.

c My bag is the blue one and hers is the red one.

d My painting won first prize, and hers won second prize.

e This pen is mine, and that one is yours.

f Jaleb took another soccer ball home after losing his at the park.

 2 **Rewrite each sentence using mine, yours, his, hers, its, ours or theirs to replace the noun groups in bold. The first one is done for you.**

a That is your book and this is **my book**.

That is your book and this is mine.

b The house on the corner is **their house**.

....

c **Our car** is the car in the carport.

....

d I put **your school bag** in the classroom.

....

e That hat is **his hat**.

....

f His answer was right but **her answer** was wrong.

....

Circle the correct pronoun to replace the words in bold in each sentence.

a	**My sister** is eleven.	He	It	She
b	**The computer** crashed.	You	It	They
c	Susie met **Cassie** at the door.	her	its	them
d	During lunch **Charlotte and I** played handball.	you	we	us
e	**The excursion** was great.	It	Them	Its
f	**Blake and I** have been chosen to put up the flag.	They	We	You
g	**Sarah** is in my basketball team.	You	They	She
h	Grandma lives overseas, so I don't see **Grandma** very often.	she	her	mine

Choose the best pronoun below to fill the gaps in the sentences.

you	**I**	**we**	**they**	**he**	**she**

a Mum was late for work because .... slept in.

b Every Christmas .... give my brother a CD.

c If you listen carefully .... will hear the kookaburra laughing.

d Natalie and I were happy because .... got an early mark.

e Hamish and Hannah will be in trouble when .... get home.

f Ben will miss training because .... has to go to the dentist.

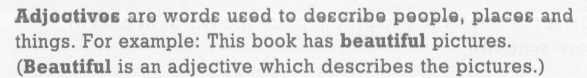

Unit 10 — Adjectives

Adjectives are words used to describe people, places and things. For example: This book has **beautiful** pictures. (**Beautiful** is an adjective which describes the pictures.)

Adjectives can also tell us about: **colour** (Nim has a **blue** board), **shape** (the biscuits are in the **round** tin), **how many** (I ate **six** biscuits) or **how much** (Pete has a **big** bag).

 1 **Circle the adjectives in each sentence. Some may have more than one adjective.**

a   We own a red car.

b   The thick fog closed the airport.

c   We had a bag of hot chips.

d   The old man had trouble climbing the steep stairs.

e   There were two cars in the garage.

f   The new plant has purple leaves.

g   In the afternoon big, black clouds came over.

h   The old door creaked as it swung open.

i   There are three hundred pupils at our school.

j   We walked down a long, narrow corridor.

k   The old tree was blown down during the fierce storm.

l   My new bike has twelve gears.

We can form adjectives from other words by adding **y** to the end of the word.

Examples:

Word	Adjective	Sentence
soap	soapy	I slipped on the **soapy** floor.
scare	scary	It was a **scary** movie.

Fill the gaps in each sentence with adjectives formed by adding y to the word in brackets.

a We watched a .... video last night. (fun)

b The old car was very .... (rust)

c Our feet were .... after the visit to the beach. (sand)

d I found the maths test .... (ease)

e Kites fly best on a .... day. (wind)

f We were very .... that the train came on time. (luck)

g The fox has a .... tail. (bush)

h Marble is often a .... white colour. (milk)

i My bedroom was .... so I had to tidy it. (mess)

j We all became .... late at night. (sleep)

k The mammoth was a very .... animal. (fur)

l Use the .... end of the stick to dig the hole. (point)

Possessive and pointing adjectives

My, your, his, her, its, our and their are adjectives which tell us who **owns** something. They are called **possessive adjectives**. For example: I rode **my** bike. (The word **my** is an adjective telling who owns the bike.)

 1 **Fill each space using the correct adjective below. The first one is done for you. One adjective is used twice.**

his	your	our	her	its	their	my

a the bag belonging to me ....*my*.... bag

b Jessica's shoe .... shoe

c Mr Herron's car .... car

d Liam and Samantha's sister .... sister

e the bone belonging to the dog .... bone

f the party held by my sister and I .... party

g the homework that you have done .... homework

h the snake's fangs .... fangs

 2 **Circle the correct word in brackets in each sentence.**

a I picked up (hers / my / me) present from under the tree.

b Stephanie lost (her / his / our) bus pass.

c Maria and Josie watched (they / them / their) paper aeroplane sail through the principal's window.

d The cat licked (their / it / its) bowl clean.

e Please leave (your / yours / you're) shoes at the door.

f Noah painted (us / their / his) skateboard yellow.

> **This**, **these**, **that** and **those** are adjectives that point out something. They are called **pointing adjectives**. For example: I carried **these** pumpkins.

Underline the pointing adjectives in each sentence.

a I will ride this bike to the party.

b Jamie's dog chewed that bone.

c These zookeepers look after the gorillas.

d That house is the one that we used to live in.

e Those pencils need to be sharpened.

f These boys will clean up the playground after lunch.

Write the pointing adjective (this, these, that or those) in each sentence and the noun it points to. The first one is done for you.

Sentence	Pointing adjective	Points to (noun)
a Justin likes these biscuits.	these	biscuits
b This ferry is going to Manly.		
c Do you like these shoes?		
d I thought that movie was boring.		
e I wonder if those bushwalkers have been found yet.		
f This book is the best one ever written.		
g How long ago did those cards go missing?		
h I don't like those new songs.		

Unit 12

Comparing adjectives

Adjectives can be used to compare two or more things. For example: I have a **bigger** piece of cake than Stephen.

Adjectives which **compare** are called **comparing adjectives**. To compare two things we add **er** (This is the tall**er** building of the two). To compare more than two things we add **est** (This is the tall**est** building in the city).

1 **Fill in the table with the correct form of comparing adjective. The first one is done for you.**

sharp	*sharper*	*sharpest*
small	....	....
strong	....	....
weak	....	....
neat	....	....
....	brighter	....
....	....	thickest
large	....	....
....	....	keenest
lucky	....	....
....	....	funniest
sad	....	....
happy	....	....

2 **Fill the gaps in each sentence with the best comparing adjective**

bigger	longer	tallest	saddest	stronger	coldest
		longest	taller		

a "Today is the .... day of my life," she sobbed.

b The fish I caught is a bit .... than yours.

c The diplodocus was the .... dinosaur.

d The weightlifter proved that he was .... than the other competitors.

e Jake is 175 centimetres tall, but Sophie is even ....

f Centrepoint Tower is the .... building in Australia.

g July is the .... month of the year.

h Each night is .... as winter approaches.

Not all comparing adjectives end in **er** or **est**. Sometimes you can use **more** or **most** before an adjective. Other adjectives change their form.

Examples: That is the **most beautiful** picture.
That picture is **more beautiful** than the other one.

My handwriting is **worse** than Jack's.
I have the **worst** handwriting in my class.

Circle the correct comparing adjective in each sentence.

a I think Vincent's drawing is (good / better / best) than my drawing.

b That is the (bad / worse / worst) movie I have ever seen.

c This problem is (confusing / more confusing / most confusing) than the one we did yesterday.

d My mum says she has the (most helpful / more helpful / helpful) children she could wish for.

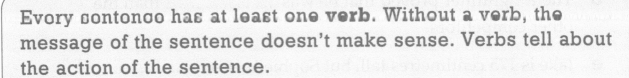

Verbs

Every sentence has at least one **verb**. Without a verb, the message of the sentence doesn't make sense. Verbs tell about the action of the sentence.

Example: Sally netball.
This message doesn't make sense. It needs a verb.
Sally **plays** netball.
Now the message makes sense.

1 **Underline the verbs (doing words) in each sentence. The first one is done for you.**

a   The painter <u>painted</u> the roof.

b   The deer ran away.

c   The dog chased the car.

d   I cooked tea.

e   Last night we watched a video.

f   I catch fish.

g   Bianca scores many goals.

h   I wear a hat to school.

2 **Choose the best verb to complete each sentence.**

falls	croak	drink	drive	hop
flies	ride	rumbles		

a   Frogs ....

b   A kite ....

e   You can .... water.

f   Thunder ....

c You can .... horses.   **g** Drivers .... cars.

d Kangaroos ....   **h** Rain ....

Saying and thinking words are also verbs.

Examples: 'Pass the tomato sauce, please,' **said** Scott.

Rebecca **thought** it was lunchtime.

Circle the saying or thinking verbs in each sentence.

a Maria thought it was time for the movie to start.

b I said that I was too tired to go on.

c Emma asked if she could go to the sick bay.

d "Look out!" shouted Mum.

e I think the price of food in the canteen is too high.

f "I forgot to bring my library book," groaned Ben.

g My father says that we should go home soon.

h Tran believed that he had done well in the test.

Relating words are also verbs.

Examples: The honey **is** runny.

I **am** a boy.

Circle the verbs (relating words) in each sentence.

a Brianne is hungry.

b We were in a hurry.

c We are all in the same class.

d My teacher was not at school.

e Sophie and Aden are very good at computers.

f Last year there were many wet days.

g My dad is a great cook.

h Yesterday was rainy and windy

Unit 14   Past tense verbs

Verbs change to match the time something happens. To show something happened in the past we often add **ed** to the end of a verb. (If a word ends in a silent **e**, drop the **e** before adding **ed**.)

Example: I **played** soccer. (The action happened in the **past**.
This is called the **past** tense.)

1 **Form the past tense of the verbs below by adding ed. The first one is done for you.**

Present tense	Past tense	Present tense	Past tense
I race	I	I laugh	I ....
I arrive	I	I walk	I ....
I chase	I	I like	I ....
I skip	I	I wrap	I ....
I copy	I	I enjoy	I ....
I collect	I	I hurry	I ....
I giggle	I	I hate	I ....
I wish	I	I hope	I ....

Some verbs change form to show that something happened in the past.

Example: I **swim** at the pool.
This action is happening **now**
(**present tense**).

Change form: I **swam** at the pool.
This action happened in the **past**
(**past tense**).

Complete the table with the past tense of the verbs.
The first one is done for you.

Present tense	Past tense	Present tense	Past tense
I freeze	I _froze_	I write	I ....
I sing	I	I ring	I ....
I see	I	I wear	I ....
I catch	I	I am	I ....
I have	I	I eat	I ....
I meet	I	I drink	I ....

Circle the correct form of the verb to fill in the gaps.

a Last week I ----- two goals.   score   scoring   scored

b The train ----- three minutes ago.   arriving   arrives   arrived

c I am ----- to the shops.   walker   walked   walking

d Last year we ----- harder.   try   tried   trying

e We ----- our cattle at the show.   showed   shown   showing

f Luke ----- lots of fruit.   eat   eats   eating

g My favourite colour ----- purple.   is   are   were

h I ----- a pie this morning.   bought   buyed   buy

i I ----- the cat last night.   feed   fed   feeding

j Yesterday Madeleine ----- the lawn.   mow   mowed   mown

k The helicopter ----- across the island
and landed.   fly   flies   flew

l The runaway van was ----- by
the guardrail.   stop   stopped   stopping

Review 2

1   Personal pronouns: me, you, her, him, it, us, you, them

Circle the correct personal pronoun to replace the words in bold type in each sentence.

a	Mum drove **Ben** to school.	him	it	he
b	**Stephanie** showed Simon the way to the office.	Her	She	They
c	We wrapped **the present** in colourful paper is leaking.	you	they	it
d	Maddie met **Josh, Tran and me** at the pool.	them	us	we

2   Possessive pronouns

Underline the possessive pronoun in each sentence.

a   The blue house is theirs.

b   My dog is the Labrador and hers is the poodle.

c   My shot went wide, but his went into the goal.

d   I left my pen at home. May I please use yours?

3   Adjectives: words that describe

Circle the adjective in each sentence.

a   Tomorrow will be a cool day.

b   The young girl is playing handball.

c   The ground was covered with a thick layer of frost.

d   Watch out for the purple monster.

4   More adjectives

Circle the correct word in brackets in each sentence.

a   Emma lost (her / its / she) library book.

b   Taylor and Josie pushed (they / them / their) bikes to the bike rack.

Underline the pointing adjective in this sentence

c   That car is the one that we used to own.

5   Comparing adjectives

Circle the correct comparing adjective in each sentence.

a   I am a (fastest / faster / fast) runner than my father.

b   That is a (good / better / best) book than the one I read last week.

c   This is the (small / smallest / smaller) kitten in the litter.

Verbs

Choose the best verb from the box to complete each sentence.

fly	roar	sing	flashes

a Lions ....

b Lightning .... in the sky.

c Entertainers often ....

d Aeroplanes ....

Verbs tell the time: past tense

Circle the correct form of the verb to fill the gaps.

a Last week I .... to the swimming pool.   running   run   ran

b I .... an egg for breakfast.   boiled   boil   boiling

c My soccer team .... the semi-final.   win   won   winner

d The plane .... half an hour ago.   departs   departure   departed

Challenge

Find an example of each of the following in the passage below. Colour each a different colour.

- number adjective
- possessive adjective
- pointing adjective
- comparing adjective

The three pigs were terrified. Not only was the Big Bad Wolf knocking loudly at their door, but the Wicked Witch was on the roof trying to find the chimney, and the giant was climbing down the giant beanstalk nearby.

"That giant looks very angry," said one pig. "It's the meanest giant I've ever seen."

REVIEW 2 SELF-ASSESSMENT	Rate your progress		
	Needs work	Good effort	Fantastic
Personal pronouns	☆	☆☆	☆☆☆
Possessive pronouns	☆	☆☆	☆☆☆
Adjectives	☆	☆☆	☆☆☆
Verbs	☆	☆☆	☆☆☆
Highlight questions you would like to revise.			

Unit 15
Verbs showing time

Verbs change according to whether an action is happening now (**present tense**) or happened in the past (**past tense**). We can also use **helping verbs** to show when an action is happening.

Examples: Alice **is watching** a video.

The action is happening **now**. (**present tense**)

Alice **was watching** a video.

The action happened in the **past**. (**past tense**)

Alice **will be watching** a video.

The action will happen in the **future**. (**future tense**)

1 **Fill in the gaps using different helping verbs to show the time. The first one is done for you.**

Present	Past	Future
I **am** eating.	I _was_ eating.	I _will be_ eating.
Joe **is** swimming.	Joe .... swimming.	Joe .... swimming.
They **are** painting.	They .... painting.	They .... painting.
You **are** riding.	You .... riding.	You .... riding.
I **am** racing.	I .... racing.	I .... racing.
We **are** cooking.	We .... cooking.	We .... cooking.

2 **Write past, present or future on the lines to show the tense of each sentence.**

a Yesterday the sun did not come out at all. ....

b The cows wandered onto the road because the gate was left open. ....

c I am writing a recount of our trip to the show. ....

d Tomorrow we will have a handball competition. ....

e Luke is eating an ice-cream. ....

f We will go shopping for Christmas presents. ....

Rewrite each sentence, changing it so the action takes place in the future. The first one is done for you.

a I wrote a letter.

I will write a letter.

b Anna rode her horse.

....

c Felicity put the photo in the album.

....

d The new library was opened by the mayor.

....

e We packed our bags very quickly.

....

f Nick told Sophie about the homework.

....

Circle the past tense verb that best fills the gap in each sentence.

a My family ----- to Queensland last year.   go / went / are going

b I ----- a picture for the   painted / will paint / am painting
class display.

c The water ----- too cold for swimming.   is / will be / was

d Ben ----- that movie last week.   saw / is seeing / may see

e Sarah ----- in a different netball team   plays / will play / played
last year.

f Our teacher   us a story.   tell / told / telling

Verbs that agree

Verbs (doing words) and their **subjects** (the person or thing doing the action) must agree. Look below to see how the verb **to be** changes to agree with the **subject**.

Singular	*Plural*
I am	we are
she is	they are
the dog is	the dogs are

1 **Cross out the verb that does not agree with the subject in each sentence.**

a Gemma (am / is) on holidays in New Zealand.

b I (am / are) in Year 3 at school.

c You (are / am) on my toe!

d My class (is / are) in the library.

e We (is / are) on our way to the pool for the school swimming carnival.

f The buses (is / are) in the car park at the side of the school.

2 **Circle the correct verb.**

a My father's office (am / is / are) on the fourteenth floor of the building.

b The windows (is / are / am) dirty after the dust storm.

c There (am / is / are) sixteen eggs in the basket.

d Where (am / is / are) your jumper?

e I (am / is / are) not sure of the answer to this puzzle.

f The cake (am / is / are) ready.

g Our train (am / is / are) already at the station.

h We (am / is / are) in the control tower at the airport.

Cross out the verb that does not agree with the subject.

a My dog (loves / love) going for a walk in the park.

b Ice-cream (melt / melts) very quickly on hot days.

c Balloons (pops / pop) if you blow too much air into them.

d Steve (have / has) two budgerigars.

e My grandfather's clock (doesn't / do not) have a battery.

f Waves often (crash / crashes) over the breakwater during a storm.

Circle the correct verb.

a The keys ----- in the drawer of my desk.   is / am / are

b Joel ----- in the house opposite mine.   live / lives

c My horse ----- pieces of apple.   enjoys / enjoy

d Where ----- my shoes?   am / are / is

e This machine ----- the bottles clean.   wash / washes

f The towels ----- still wet.   are / am / is

g Nim ----- the lunch orders every day.   collect / collects

h We ----- just enough time for a snack before we leave. have / has

Contractions

Contractions are joined words with a letter or letters missing. An apostrophe is put in the place of the missing letter or letters. For example: is not / **isn't**

Many contractions are formed from a verb and the word **not**. The letter **o** is dropped from **not** and replaced with an apostrophe.

1 **Write the contractions on the lines below. The first one is done for you.**

was not	_wasn't_	did not	....
could not	....	does not	....
do not	....	have not	....
has not	....	were not	....
are not	....	would not	....
is not	....	had not	....

Take care with:

| will not | .... | can not | .... |

I won't move!

Contractions can also be formed from other words. For example: I am / **I'm**

2 **Write the contractions on the lines below. The first one is done for you.**

I had	_I'd_	you are	....
there is	....	here is	....
I will	....	you had	....

they would	....	he is	....
she had	....	you have	....
you will	....	that is	....

Cross out the incorrect contraction in the brackets. The first one is done for you.

a You (aren't / ~~are'nt~~ / ~~arn't~~) the only person to be early.

b "(I'd / I'had / I'ad) better go," said Joshua.

c Alex says (she'es / she's / shes') very hungry.

d (Whats' / Whant's / What's) for breakfast?

e Rachael (has'nt / haven't / hasn't) brought her lunch.

f (Thats' / That's / Tha'ts) is my bike.

Circle the correct contraction for the words in bold text.

a **He is** reading a book in his room.   She's   It's   He's

b **Where is** my pencil?   Whereis   Where's   Wheres'

c **There is** a spider on the ceiling.   Their's   Ther's   There's

d **I have** left the biggest piece for you.   I 've   Iv'e   You've

e I **have not** seen your sister today.   have not   hav'nt   haven't

f There **are not** enough chairs for everyone.   isn't   aren't   are'nt

g Paola **could not** find her books.   could't   couldn't   couldnt'

h The visitors **have not** arrived yet.   have'nt   haven't   havent

i **There is** the finish line!   Their's   Theres   There's

Adverbs are words that tell us more about an action.

Example: Petra walked **slowly**.

The word **slowly** is an adverb that tells us how Petra walked. Adverbs often end in **ly**.

1 Circle the adverb in each sentence and write the verb it describes. The first one is done for you.

a The girl raced (quickly) along the track. .....*raced*.....

b I smiled happily when I opened my presents. ....

c The cat glared angrily at the dog. ....

d A storm came suddenly at teatime. ....

e The thunder rumbled noisily as the rain fell. ....

f The man shouted crossly at the dog. ....

g The snow fell silently from the sky. ....

h My dog eagerly wagged its tail. ....

i I broke the plate accidentally. ....

j Mela won the race easily. ....

k I stumbled wearily at the end of the race. ....

We can form adverbs from other words by adding **ly**.

Examples: loud / loudly

The cat purred **loudly**.

Fill the gaps with adverbs formed by adding ly to the word in brackets.

a The truck roared ....   (loud)

b The snow fell .... onto the roof.   (soft)

c I could see the city .... from the lookout.   (clear)

d My teacher shook his head .... as he looked
at my model.   (sad)

e I can write ....   (neat)

f Put the plates away ....   (careful)

g Kyle shouted ....   (sudden)

h If you hold your pencil ...., your handwriting
will improve.   (correct)

It is a common mistake to use an adjective instead of an adverb.

Circle the correct word in brackets.

a I ran (quick / quickly) in my race at the school carnival.

b There are lots of (quick / quickly) readers in my class.

c We shouted (loud / loudly) but no-one
answered.

d A (loud / loudly) crash of thunder made
me jump.

e Zac wrote his name (carefully / careful) on
the line.

f Pete is a (carefully / careful) drawer.

g The vet stroked the injured animal
(gently / gentle).

h A (gently / gentle) breeze began to blow.

Unit 19 More about adverbs

Adverbs can tell us **how** an action is done.

1 Circle the **how** adverbs in each sentence.

a   Mr Pascoe quickly handed out the notes.

b   Habib knocked gently on the door.

c   We looked carefully through the boxes for the missing book.

d   The damaged plane landed safely at the airport.

e   Kyle glared angrily at the intruder.

f   The sun shone brightly all day.

Adverbs can tell us **when** an action happens or happened.

Example: I wrote to Brittany **yesterday**.

(**yesterday** is an adverb telling **when** I wrote to Brittany)

2 Circle the **when** adverbs in each sentence.
Write the verb each one describes on the line.

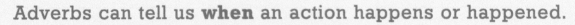

a   Jessica leaves tomorrow.   ....

b   Yesterday we went to the beach.   ....

c   I feed my pets daily.   ....

d   We go to the movies tonight.   ....

e   The bells ring hourly.   ....

f   We visited a museum today.   ....

Adverbs can tell us **where** an action is done.

Examples: I wrote my name **there**. (**there** is an adverb telling **where** I
wrote my name)

Circle the where adverbs in each sentence. Underline the verbs they describe.

a Jack put the ball down.

b We ran outside.

c I left my bag inside.

d The plane circled above for a few minutes.

e The sailors went below after their watch.

f My bedroom is upstairs.

Circle the adverbs in each sentence. Underline the verbs they describe. Write on the line whether the adverb is a how, when or where adverb.

a The goldfish swam lazily around the fish tank. ....

b We went downstairs. ....

c My brother laughed loudly when I told him the joke. ....

d We went to the supermarket yesterday. ....

e Our assembly is held weekly. ....

f The fog hid the buildings in the city completely. ....

Unit 20

Prepositions

Prepositions are little words such as **before** and **under**, which tell about time and place. They are placed in front of nouns and pronouns to link them with other words in a sentence.

Examples: We went home **after** the movie. (**after** is a preposition linking movie to home — it tells us about **time**)

We found the kitten **inside** a box. (**inside** is a preposition linking box to kitten — it tells us about **place**)

Other common prepositions are: **out**, **along**, **up**, **down**, **before**, **after**, **in**, **through**, **beside** and **on**.

1 **Underline the prepositions in each sentence. The first one is done for you.**

a The stick floated <u>under</u> the bridge.

b The horse jumped over the fence.

c The bottles were knocked off the shelf.

d Liana raced through the door.

e I waited beside the main gate.

f Our farm is near a large town.

g Lim handed the present to Katie.

h We scrubbed the dirty marks off the wall.

i Pia put the flowers in a vase.

j The lizard lay basking on a rock in the sun.

k The children hid behind the fence.

l I patted the dog in the kennel.

m They ate all the chips from the packet.

n We cooked pasta on the stove.

Fill the gaps in the sentences with a suitable preposition. The first one is done for you.

up	between	during	into	in	of
	across	behind	to	against	

a The baby bird took shelter .... the nest.

b We jumped .... gap in the floor.

c Alex hid .... the shed.

d The bat was leaning .... the chair.

e Bella sat .... Maria and Nikki.

f There has been no rain .... April.

g Joel put the mixture .... the cake tin.

h The truck struggled .... the steep grade .... the top .... the hill.

Circle the correct preposition in the brackets.

a There were presents for everyone (over / under) the tree.

b I live (in / at) Sydney.

c It was too hot to go (at / to) the beach yesterday.

d I sit (at / in) my desk to do my homework.

e My dog is afraid (by / of) horses.

f Everyone will be able to take part (at / in) the play.

g Can you help me look (to / for) my pencil?

h My big brother is (on / in) high school.

i The horses ate all the grass (in / off) the paddock.

j My doctor took my temperature (with / from) a thermometer

k The sheep escaped (from / out) the pen

An **adverbial phrase** is a group of words telling us **where**, **when**, **how** or **with whom** an action is done. It does not contain a verb. Phrases often begin with a preposition such as **out**, **in**, **along**, **with** or **on**.

1 **Circle the adverbial phrase that tells where in each sentence.**

Example: I wrote my name in the book. (**in the book** is an adverbial phrase telling **where** I wrote)

a I put the box on the shelf.

b The bus struggled up the steep road.

c Dad hung the washing on the line.

d Mrs Taylor wrote the exercise on the board.

e I gave my dog a wash in the backyard.

f I have a computer at home.

2 **Circle the adverbial phrase that tells when in each sentence.**

Example: I saw Sam in the afternoon. (**in the afternoon** is an adverbial phrase telling **when** I saw Sam)

a We went to the pool in the morning.

b After dinner I read a book.

c Sarah feeds the chickens before breakfast.

d On Wednesdays my class goes to the library.

e Pia visited Sally during the holidays.

f The cake was cooked after forty minutes.

Circle the adverbial phrase that tells how in each sentence.

Example: I wrote my name in my best printing (**in my best printing** is an adverbial phrase telling **how** I wrote my name).

a   Jarred spoke with an angry voice.

b   The tree fell with a mighty crash.

c   With great care the ranger picked up the frightened animal.

d   Jo swallowed the cake in one gulp.

e   The wind blew the door shut with a bang.

f   Tom held the reins with a firm hand.

Circle the adverbial phrase that tells with whom in each sentence.

Example: I went to the pool with my mother (**with my mother** is an adverbial phrase telling **with whom** I went to the pool).

a   I went to the beach with my family.

b   Ben had a game with Xian.

c   We went to the show with my grandmother.

d   The students went with their teachers to the assembly.

e   Steve catches the bus to school with me.

f   My dog likes to run around in the park with other dogs.

Review 3

1 Past tense

Circle the verbs that show past tense

a	The train .... running late.	is	will be	was
b	The lion .... to the waterhole for a drink.	will go	went	are going
c	My father and I .... a movie.	saw	are seeing	may see

2 Using verbs that agree

Cross out the verb that does not agree with the subject in each sentence.

a Five canaries (is / are) in the cage.

b Brittany (am / is) the best runner in the school.

c The team (is / are) leading the competition.

3 Contractions

Circle the correct contraction

a	I have arrived at school on time.	I've	Iv'e	You've
b	She is playing soccer with her friends.	She's	She'll	He's
c	There is a new computer in my classroom.	Their's	Ther's	There's
d	Where is the other set of stumps?	Whereis	Where's	Wheres'

4 Adverbs and adjectives

Circle the correct word in brackets.

a The mouse made a (soft / softly) squeak as it scampered across the room.

b We whispered (soft / softly).

c We crept (silent / silently) into the room.

d She gave a (silent / silently) signal for the others to keep quiet.

5 More about adverbs: words that tell us about actions

Circle the **how** adverbs. Underline the verb each one describes.

a Matt quickly returned the ball.

Circle the **when** adverbs in each sentence. Underline the verb each one describes

b Our bus leaves later.

Circle the **where** adverbs in each sentence. Underline the verb each one describes.

c The dog came inside.

d We ran downstairs.

Prepositions: words that tell about time and place

Fill the gaps in the sentences with a suitable preposition from the box.

up	during	across	against

a I leant my bike .... the tree.

b We left .... the show.

c We rolled the barrel .... the hall.

Adverbial phrases: groups of words that tell more about actions

Circle the adverbial phrase that tells **where** in this sentence.

a We found the pool toys in the garage.

Circle the adverbial phrase that tells **when** in this sentence.

b Before lunch we had a swim.

Circle the adverbial phrase that tells **how** in this sentence.

c We lifted the injured bird with great care.

Circle the adverbial phrase that tells **with whom** in this sentence.

d My cat never plays with other cats.

Challenge

Find examples of each of the following in the passage below. Colour each a different colour.

- an adverbial phrase that tells with whom
- three contractions
- an adverbial phrase that tells when
- an adverb
- an adjective

Have you ever had to put something away that someone else has left carelessly lying around? Do you think this is fair? I don't.

It's easy to forget to put toys and other things away after playtime. But imagine what your classroom would look like if no-one put anything away after they'd finished with them! It is important to clean up after ourselves. Sometimes it's even fun to clean up with your best friends.

REVIEW 3 SELF-ASSESSMENT	Rate your progress		
	Needs work	Good effort	Fantastic
Verb tenses	☆	☆☆	☆☆☆
Contractions	☆	☆☆	☆☆☆
Adverbs, adjectives, prepositions	☆	☆☆	☆☆☆
Adverbial phrases	☆	☆☆	☆☆☆
Highlight questions you would like to revise.			

Clauses

A **clause** is a group of words that tells us about an action and the people or things involved. Clauses always contain a verb. Clauses have a **subject** — the person or thing doing the action of the verb — and they usually have an **object** — the person or thing receiving the action of the verb.

Example: Paolo   hit   the ball
                subject   *verb*   *object*

1   **Write the verbs from the following clauses on the lines The first one has been done for you.**

a   The boat sailed across the water.   *sailed*

b   We saw the game on television.   ....

c   Sausages sizzled on the barbecue.   ....

d   Many people visited school today.   ....

e   School finishes at three o'clock.   ....

f   Snow swirled around us.   ....

g   You have my bag.   ....

h   Snow sometimes falls in Canberra.   ....

i   Lightning struck a tree in the park.   ....

j   The plane landed on the airstrip.   ....

Circle the subject in the following clauses. (Hint: ask yourself who or what is doing the action. For example, in question a, ask "What arrived?" Answer: The train.)

a (The train) arrived at the station.

b Priam ate the icing first.

c Our team lost the final.

d Emily put on her raincoat.

e The cups rattled in the cupboard.

f The driver parked the truck.

g Mr Truscott read the note.

h The horses galloped around the paddock.

i Adam dived into the pool.

j My cousins live in Canada.

Write the object of the following clauses on the lines. (Hint: ask yourself who or what is receiving the action. For example, in question a, ask: My cat licked what? Answer: The cream.)

a My cat licked the cream.   *the cream*

b Alice caught the ball.   ....

c Mani wrote that story.   ....

d Ben scratched his back.   ....

e The sun dried our wet clothes.   ....

f The wave hit Tom.   ....

g The horse ate the apple.   ....

h Rainwater filled the bucket.   ....

i The bushfire destroyed five houses.   ....

j Rachael is wearing a purple jacket.   ....

Unit 23 · Simple sentences

A **simple sentence** has just one clause that makes sense on its own. For example: I ran along the road.

Checkpoint! A clause is a group of words that tells us about an action and people or things involved. A clause always contains a verb.

1 Unjumble the words to make simple sentences and write them on the lines. Remember to put a capital letter at the beginning of the sentence and a full stop at the end. Circle the verb.

a breakfast I ate   I (ate) breakfast.

b went home we   ....

c quiet the is class   ....

d water warm feels the   ....

e dived Jack board the off   ....

f new loved puppy her Kristi   ....

g bike has Anil a blue   ....

h shop Lucas at ice-cream brought the an   ....

i plane sky the the in high flew   ....

j flowed the slowly stream   ....

There are four types of sentences.

- **Statements** tell about something. Statements begin with a capital letter and end with a full stop. (For example: I am walking to town.)

- **Questions** ask something. Questions begin with a capital letter and end with a question mark. (For example: Are you walking to town?)

- **Exclamations** express something strongly. Exclamations begin with a capital letter and end with an exclamation mark. (For example: Help!)

- **Commands** are short statements that tell someone or something to act in a certain way. Commands begin with a capital letter and end with a full stop.
  (For example: Come here.)

Write statement, question, exclamation or command after each sentence.

a Jo couldn't see her sister.   _statement_

b Watch out!   ....

c Where is your book?   ....

d Take your hat off.   ....

e May I watch the game?   ....

f The storm lasted for only
   fifteen minutes.   ....

g We visited my uncle last Christmas. ....

h Where is the stadium?   ....

i Stop!   ....

j Turn the tap off.   ....

Unit 24 Joining sentences

The words **and**, **but** and **or** are joining words. They can be used to join simple sentences. For example, the sentences "Peta rides her bike to school. I catch the bus", can be written as "Peta rides her bike to school **but** I catch the bus".

Checkpoint!   Joining words like **and**, **but** and **or** are called **conjunctions**.

1 **Join the simple sentences with and, but or or. Choose the conjunction which best fits the sentence.**

a I like netball. Cassie prefers hockey.

....

b Turn off the oven. The cake will burn.

....

c The lights dimmed. The concert began.

....

d I tried to print my story. There was no paper in the printer.

....

e The bridge opened. The boat sailed through.

....

f The waves became much bigger. Most of the people left the water.

....

g My house is made of wood. Sally's house is made of brick.

....

h Be careful. You may spill your drink.

....

Divide the following sentences into two simple sentences. Leave out the conjunction. The first one is done for you.

a I ate one sausage but I couldn't manage two.

I ate one sausage. I couldn't manage two.

b The wind blew very strongly and some of the sailing boats tipped over.

....

....

c I like apples but Ben prefers grapes.

....

....

d Finish that sheet quickly or there will be no time for a story.

....

....

e We sat on the floor and Mrs Martinez handed out the notes.

....

....

f Alex remembered his boots but he forgot his T-shirt.

....

....

g I knocked on the door but Mr Hill did not answer.

....

....

h The tap must be turned off firmly or it will drip.

....

....

Unit 25

Punctuating sentences

Thore are four types of sentences: **statements**, **questions**, **exclamations** and **commands**. Each has its own punctuation rules. (See Unit 23.)

1 **Rewrite each statement using the correct punctuation.**

a we made masks at school

....

b the jellies are set

....

c three friends came to my party

....

d my room has two windows

....

e my swimming lesson is on Saturday

....

2 **Rewrite each question using the correct punctuation.**

a how old are you

....

b can you tell me where the pool is

....

c how much do the ice-creams cost

....

d what is the name of that animal

....

e where are your shoes

....

Rewrite each exclamation using the correct punctuation.

a stop ....

b jump ....

c duck ....

d ouch ....

e we won ....

Rewrite each command using the correct punctuation.

a open your books ....

b do not open your presents ....

c wash your hands ....

d bring your work to me ....

e put down your paintbrushes ....

Rewrite each sentence using the correct punctuation.

a where is Stefan ....

b pass the ball to Erica ....

c that is a kookaburra ....

d who is that ....

e what a surprise ....

Unit 26 — Capital letters and commas

Capital letters are used in the following places:

- at the start of every sentence

- the first letter of a proper noun and the title of a special person (eg: the **Prime Minister**)

- the title of a book, play, film, song (eg: '**Advance Australian Fair**')

- a heading (eg: **The Life and Times of Francis Greenway**) (Small words such as **and**, **of** and **the** do not usually have capital letters in titles and headings unless they are the first word of the title.)

- the personal pronoun I (eg: **I** don't think **I'**ll go to the show because **I'**m feeling ill)

- in direct speech (see Unit 27).

1 **Circle the words which should have capitals in each sentence.**

a canberra is the capital city of australia.

b i go to soccer practice on tuesday and play my game on saturday.

c the murray river is the longest river in australia.

d my teacher's name is mrs jackson.

e the smallest planet in the solar system is pluto.

f my best friend's name is alice.

g the swan river flows through perth.

h fraser island lies off the coast of queensland.

i where is mark?

j i don't think i have played marbles before.

k my favourite book is the magic pudding.

l mayor judi roberts opened the school fete.

Commas are used to separate items in a list of nouns, adjectives or adverbs, and to indicate direct speech (see unit 27).

Checkpoint! There is usually no comma after the second last item in a list if it is followed by **and**. Example: I brought watermelon, oranges, apples **and** pears.

Put commas in the correct places in each sentence.

a My favourite fruits are watermelon grapes bananas and pears.

b Don't forget to bring your swimmers a towel a hat and a spare T-shirt.

c I invited Hani Jo Max and Andre to my party.

d We cooked the sausages prawns and kebabs on the barbecue.

e The four largest planets in our solar system are Jupiter Saturn Neptune and Uranus.

f There were green red blue and yellow flags hanging on the buildings.

g Slowly carefully and quietly Jani opened the door.

h Issac ate two kebabs a steak two bread rolls and a bowl of salad.

i My new jumper has red yellow and black stripes on the sleeves.

j The scores were seven four six two eight and five.

Direct speech

When we write the actual words someone says, it is called **direct speech**. The following examples show the correct punctuation for direct speech.

> *speech marks*   *speech marks*
>
> "See   you   tomorrow,"   Paul said.
>
> *capital letter*   *comma inside the speech marks*   *full stop*

>   *speech marks*   *speech marks*
>
> The driver said,   "Move to the back of the bus, please."
>
> *comma*   *capital letter to begin speech*   *full stop*

1   **Put the speech marks around the direct speech in each sentence**

   a   Are you ready? asked Mum.

   b   That's my red pencil, said Gusta.

   c   Marc called, Pass me the ball.

   d   There are no more biscuits left, replied Josie.

   e   We'll meet this afternoon, agreed Issac.

   f   Perhaps you could tidy your room, suggested Dad.

2   **Put commas and full stops in the correct places in each sentence**

   a   "Dinner will ready in five minutes" said Dad

   b   Justin replied "The pencil sharpener is on my desk"

   c   "This is a great book" remarked Sam

   d   "We went to Melbourne in the holidays" said Franca

   e   "Be careful to hold your ruler steady" advised Mr Grant

   f   Nim said "I like strawberry ice-cream best"

Circle the letters which should be capitals in each sentence.

a "where is your jacket?" asked mum.

b jessica replied, "yes, that is my bag."

c "may i have some tomato sauce, please?" asked ben.

d "i have two guinea pigs," boasted rachael.

e dad commented, "this is the oldest building in our town."

f "perhaps you have eaten too much chocolate," suggested grandma.

Rewrite each sentence, including speech marks, commas, capital letters and full stops.

a there are apples in the fridge said mum

....

....

b here is my hat said joel

....

....

c ethan declared i am nine today.

....

....

Punctuation practice

1 **Some punctuation marks are missing from these sentences. Circle the best punctuation mark to fill the gap.**

a When is your birthday ---   ,   .   ?

b Look out ---   .   !   ?

c "Have you found your book --- asked Mr Dizan.   ,"   ?"   .

d We have horses --- cows and goats on our farm.   .   ,   "

e The latch on the gate is broken ---   ,   .   !

f "This is my classroom --- remarked Jessie.   ,"   ",   ."

g "The photos of the excursion have arrived ---   ."   ?"   "!
said Mr Cox.

h "What a great shot --- cried Mrs Anderson.   !   ."   !"

2 **Each of these sentences has one punctuation mistake. Rewrite each sentence correctly and draw a red circle around the punctuation you changed.**

a my favourite computer game is Fantasy Forest.

....

....

b The largest city in Australia is Sydney?

....

....

c "What's the matter," asked Nadia.

....

....

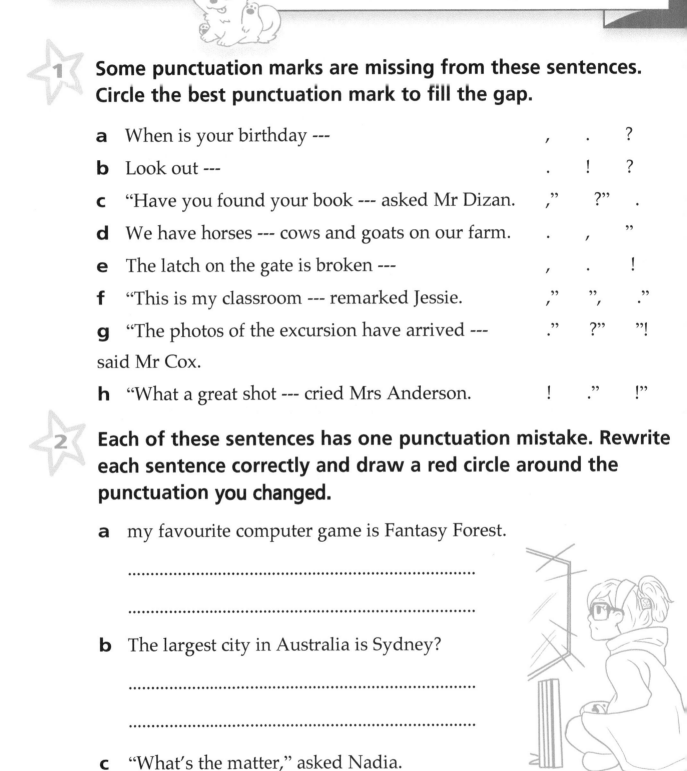

Rewrite each sentence using the correct punctuation.

a that hat belongs to jason

....

b have you any library books to return

....

c here is the lid of the box

....

d stop

....

e last year in august i visited the great barrier reef

....

....

f i have my own dictionary at home

....

g ouch cried Zoe

....

h turn the television off said dad

....

Review 4

1   **What makes up a clause?**

Write the verbs from the following clauses on the lines. Draw a box around the subject. Colour the object.

a   Paolo kicked the ball.   ....

b   The falling branch hit our house   ....

2   **Sentences**

Write whether each sentence is a statement, question, exclamation or command.

a   We have sport every Friday.   ....

b   Help!   ....

c   What is the time?   ....

d   Sit down.   ....

3   **Joining sentences**

Join the following simple sentences with **and, but** or **or**. Choose the one which best fits the sentence.

a   The shark alarm sounded. Everybody left the water.

....

b   Put on your goggles. The water may sting your eyes.

....

c   I wanted to go to my friend's place. Mum wouldn't let me.

....

4   **Punctuating sentences**

Rewrite each statement using the correct punctuation. You will need to decide first if the sentence is a statement, a question, an exclamation or a command.

a   we went to the football match ....

b   is the toast ready ....

c   watch out ....

d   put the stick down ....

e   what do you want to do ....

f   watch this show ....

Punctuation: capital letters; commas

Circle the words which should have capitals in each sentence.

a mount kosciuszko is the highest mountain in australia.

b i saw mr fulton in bellbrook last saturday

Put commas in the correct places in the sentence.

c During the holidays we visited Swan Hill Deniliquin Mildura and Wentworth.

Punctuation: direct speech

Rewrite each sentence, including speech marks, commas, capital letters and full stops.

a you should go to the doctor said dad ....

b trina said I'm ready for school ....

Punctuation revision

Some punctuation marks are missing from these sentences. Circle the best punctuation mark to fill the gap.

a What are you doing ....   ,   .   ?

b Stop ....   !   ?

c "I want you to help me .... said Becky   ,"   ?"   .

Challenge

Use the following punctuation marks in the passage.

- 5 capital letters
- 2 full stops
- 1 question mark
- 1 exclamation mark
- 2 commas

the dentist leaned over matt's face
"oh my goodness" she exclaimed
a little later she asked "does this hurt"

REVIEW 4 SELF-ASSESSMENT	Rate your progress		
	Needs work	Good effort	Fantastic
Clauses	☆	☆☆	☆☆☆
Sentences	☆	☆☆	☆☆☆
Joining sentences	☆	☆☆☆	☆☆☆☆
Punctuation	☆	☆☆	☆☆☆
Highlight questions you would like to revise.			

Glossary

adjective	word which adds meaning to a noun or pronoun
adjectival phrase	word group which adds meaning to a noun or pronoun
adverb	word which adds meaning to a verb
adverbial phrase	word group which adds meaning to a verb
apostrophe	punctuation mark used to show ownership, and to mark the missing letters in a contraction
article	word that points to a noun or pronoun (**a**, **an** and **the** are the only articles)
bullet point	(also called **dot point**) a list where each line starts with a dot to make it stand out more
clause	word group containing a verb
collective noun	name of a group of people or things
comma (,)	punctuation mark used in a sentence to show a short pause, or to separate two parts of a sentence
command	a short statement that orders or directs a certain action
common noun	name of anything you can see, hear, smell, touch or taste
conjunction	connecting word, used to join phrases and clauses
contraction	a single word formed by joining and shortening two words, with missing letters marked by an apostrophe
direct speech	(also called **quoted speech**) the exact words someone said or thought
exclamation	a sentence that expresses surprise, strong emotion or suddenness
exclamation mark (!)	punctuation mark used at the end of an exclamation
full stop (.)	punctuation used at the end of a statement, and sometimes at the end of an abbreviation
indirect speech	(also called **reported speech**) a report what someone has said, rather than a direct quote
noun	name of a person, place or thing
object	(see **subject**) the person or thing in a sentence that "receives" the action of the verb
phrase	word group that adds meaning to a sentence, but does not contain a verb
plural	more than one
prefix	a group of letters added to the beginning of a word changing its meaning
preposition	word that shows the relationship between nouns and pronouns
pronoun	word that stands for a noun
proper noun	name of a particular person place or thing
question	a sentence that asks something
question mark (?)	punctuation mark used at the end of a question
sentence	group of words that expresses a complete thought and contains a verb
singular	one
statement	a sentence that tells or informs
subject	the person or thing that the sentence is about
suffix	a group of letters added to the beginning of a word changing its meaning
tense	form of a verb showing when the action occurred
verb	acting or being word

Answers

Unit 1

hat, book, beach, cow, girl, Jupiter, face, uncle, game, sky, triangle, brother, Peter, hamburger, Sydney

a backpack **b** apple **c** window **d** mirror
e teacher **f** shirt **g** bottle **h** desk

a woman **b** table, chairs **c** teacher, class
d canary **e** car, garage **f** books, shelf
g house, night **h** cyclone, town, buildings

a pool **b** paper **c** log **d** brush **e** truck **f** July
g piano **h** carrot

Unit 2

city, bus, country, diver, planet, mouse, river, ocean, soccer, boy, month, aeroplane, cake, holiday, state

a platypus **b** kitchen **c** wheels **d** light **e** pea
f ocean **g** disk **h** supermarket

a school, pupils **b** brother, soccer **c** rain, creek
d neighbour, car **e** teacher, ice-cream **f** can, worms
g kangaroo, plain **h** winter, snow, mountains

a dugong **b** wombat **c** bilby **d** echidna **e** koala
f potoroo **g** possum **h** crocodile

Unit 3

Tasmania, Tokyo, France, Theo, Thursday, Easter, Mt Warning, Torrens, Sally, Mediterranean, October, Emerald, Murrumbidgee, Kakadu, Phillip

a Darwin **b** Michelle, Sarah **c** Victa **d** Canberra,
Australia **e** Lang Road **f** *Blinky Bill* **g** Bass Strait,
Tasmania, Victoria **h** Alice Springs

a September **b** Parkes **c** Canberra **d** Corolla
e India **f** Pacific Ocean **g** Hume Highway
h Friday
(Check each answer is a proper noun and has a
capital letter.)

Unit 4

a crew **b** band **c** choir **d** team **e** class **f** gang

a bunch **b** swarm **c** school **d** mob **e** herd **f** batch

a hand **b** pack **c** pod **d** litter **e** flight **f** posy

squad — a group of athletes that are on tour
together
clutch — a group of chickens
audience — a group of people watching a show
convoy— a line of vehicles travelling together

pack — a group of wolves
gaggle — a group of geese
galaxy — a large group of stars
regiment — a group of soldiers
flock — a group of seagulls

Unit 5

1 monkey, cliff, baby, octopus, glass, woman, crop,
wave, drum, peach, bush, taxi

2 cities, tapes, countries, dishes, drains, buses,
circuses, packages, geese, trolleys, months,
rectangles

3 sharks, classes, kangaroos, bikes, fences,
sandwiches, buckets, insects, dishes, answers,
pieces, boxes, thumbs, wishes, surprises

4 sister, mouse, brush, poem, banana, dress, race,
handle, patch, child, tooth, fox, taxi, square, house

5 jellies, ways, birthdays, bodies, families, parties,
donkeys, holidays, lollies, berries

6 key, body, monkey, pony, ferry, fairy, boy, puppy

Unit 6

1 **a** An **b** A **c** a **d** an **e** An **f** A **g** a **h** A **i** an **j** an

2 **a** a **b** the **c** the **d** a **e** the **f** the

3 **a** (a)/ the **b** (a)/ the **c** (A)/ The **d** (the)/ a **e** (an)/ the
f (A)/ An **g** (a)/ the **h** (a)/ the **i** (an)/ a **j** (a)/ the

Unit 7

1 **a** He plays soccer. **b** They are nine. **c** She read the
book aloud. **d** They live in Canada. **e** He came to
my party. **f** It was loaded with fruit. **g** They were
stacked on the floor. **h** It disappeared down a hole.

2 **a** I **b** you **c** we

3 **a** She **b** It **c** We **d** He **e** It **f** They **g** She **h** They

4 **a** she **b** we **c** you **d** he **e** they **f** I

Unit 8

1 **a** I couldn't see them. **b** Anna wrote her a letter.
c Jacob put it in the folder. **d** I gave him a golf ball.
e We packed them very quickly. **f** David told him
the answer. **g** We visited her in the holidays.
h I left it at the pool.

2 **a** me **b** us **c** you

3 **a** us **b** her **c** him **d** it **e** them **f** it **g** her **h** it

4 **a** her **b** us **c** you **d** him **e** them **f** me

Unit 9

1 **a** yours **b** theirs **c** hers **d** hers **e** mine, yours **f** his

2 **a** That is your book and this is **mine**. **b** The house on the corner is **theirs**. **c** **Ours** is the car in the carport. **d** I put **yours** in the classroom. **e** That hat is **his**. **f** His answer was right but **hers** was wrong.

3 **a** She **b** It **c** her **d** we **e** It **f** we **g** She **h** her

4 **a** she **b** I **c** you **d** we **e** they **f** he

Unit 10

1 **a** red **b** thick **c** hot **d** old, steep **e** two **f** new, purple **g** big, black **h** old **i** three hundred **j** long, narrow **k** old, fierce **l** new, twelve

2 **a** funny **b** rusty **c** sandy **d** easy **e** windy **f** lucky **g** bushy **h** milky **i** messy **j** sleepy **k** furry **l** pointy

Unit 11

1 **a** my bag **b** her shoe **c** his car **d** their sister **e** its bone **f** our party **g** your homework **h** its fangs

2 **a** my **b** her **c** their **d** its **e** your **f** his

3 **a** this **b** that **c** These **d** That **e** Those **f** These

4 **a** these, biscuits **b** This, ferry **c** these, shoes **d** that, movie **e** those, bushwalkers **f** This, book **g** those, cards **h** those, songs

Unit 12

1 sharp, sharper, sharpest; small, smaller, smallest; strong, stronger, strongest; weak, weaker, weakest; neat, neater, neatest; bright, brighter, brightest; thick, thicker, thickest; large, larger, largest; keen, keener, keenest; lucky, luckier, luckiest; funny, funnier, funniest; sad, sadder, saddest; happy, happier, happiest

2 **a** saddest **b** bigger **c** longest **d** stronger **e** taller **f** tallest **g** coldest **h** darker

3 **a** better **b** worst **c** more confusing **d** most helpful

Unit 13

1 **a** painted **b** ran **c** chased **d** cooked **e** watched **f** catch **g** scores **h** wear

2 **a** croak **b** flies **c** ride **d** hop **e** drink **f** rumbles **g** drive **h** falls

3 **a** thought **b** said **c** asked **d** shouted **e** think **f** groaned **g** says **h** believed

4 **a** is **b** were **c** are **d** was **e** are **f** were **g** is **h** was

Unit 14

1 raced, laughed, arrived, walked, chased, liked, skipped, wrapped, copied, enjoyed, collected, hurried, giggled, hated, wished, hoped

2 froze, wrote, sang, rang, saw, wore, caught, was, had, ate, met, drank

3 **a** scored **b** arrived **c** walking **d** tried **d** showed **f** eats **g** is **h** bought **i** fed **j** mowed **k** flew **l** stopped

Unit 15

1 Joe was swimming / Joe will be swimming; They were painting / They will be painting; You were riding / You will be riding; I was racing / I will be racing; We were cooking / We will be cooking.

2 **a** past **b** past **c** present **d** future **e** present **f** future

3 **a** I will write a letter.
b Anna will ride her horse.
c Felicity will put the photo in the album.
d The new library will be opened by the mayor.
e We will pack our bags very quickly.
f Nick will tell Sophie about the homework.

4 **a** went **b** painted **c** was **d** saw **e** played **f** told

Unit 16

1 **a** is **b** am **c** are **d** is **e** are **f** are

2 **a** is **b** are **c** are **d** is **e** am **f** is **g** is **h** are

3 **a** loves **b** melts **c** pop **d** has **e** doesn't **f** crash

4 **a** are **b** lives **c** enjoys **d** are **e** washes **f** are **g** collects **h** have

Unit 17

1 wasn't, didn't, couldn't, doesn't, don't, haven't, hasn't, weren't, aren't, wouldn't, isn't, hadn't, won't, can't.

2 I'd, you're, there's, here's, I'll, you'd, they'd, he's, she'd, you've, you'll, that's.

3 **a** aren't **b** I'd **c** she's **d** What's **e** hasn't **f** That's

4 **a** He's **b** Where's **c** There's **d** I've **e** haven't **f** aren't **g** couldn't **h** haven't **i** There's

Unit 18

1 **a** quickly, raced **b** happily, smiled **c** angrily, glared **d** suddenly, came **e** noisily, rumbled **f** crossly, shouted **g** silently, fell **h** eagerly,

wagged **i** accidentally, broke **j** easily, won
k wearily, stumbled

a loudly **b** softly **c** clearly **d** sadly **e** neatly
f carefully **g** suddenly **h** correctly

a quickly **b** quick **c** loudly **d** loud **e** carefully
f careful **g** gently **h** gentle

a quickly **b** gently **c** carefully **d** safely **e** angrily
f brightly

a tomorrow, leaves **b** Yesterday, went **c** daily,
feed **d** tonight, go **e** hourly, ring **f** today, visited

a down, put **b** outside, ran **c** inside, left **d** above,
circled **e** below, went **f** upstairs, is

a lazily, swam / how **b** downstairs, went / where
c loudly, laughed / how **d** yesterday, went / when
e weekly, held / when **f** completely, hid / how

a under **b** over **c** off **d** through **e** beside **f** near
g to **h** off **i** in **j** on, in **k** behind **l** in **m** from **n** on

a in **b** across **c** behind **d** against **e** between
f during **g** into **h** up, to, of

a under **b** in **c** to **d** at **e** of **f** in **g** for **h** in **i** in
j with **k** from

a on the shelf **b** up the steep road **c** on the line
d on the board **e** in the backyard **f** at home

a in the morning **b** After dinner **c** before breakfast
d On Wednesdays **e** during the holidays **f** after
forty minutes

a with an angry voice **b** with a mighty crash
c With great care **d** in one gulp **e** with a bang
f with a firm hand

a with my family **b** with Xian **c** with my
grandmother **d** with their teachers **e** with me
f with other dogs

a sailed **b** saw **c** sizzled **d** visited **e** finishes
f swirled **g** have **h** falls **i** struck **j** landed

a The train **b** Priam **c** Our team **d** Emily **e** The
pups **f** The driver **g** Mr Truscott **h** The horses
i Adam **j** My cousins

3 a the cream **b** the ball **c** that story **d** his back
e our wet clothes **f** Tom **g** the apple **h** the bucket
i five houses **j** a purple jacket

1 a I (ate) breakfast. **b** We (went) home. **c** The class
(is) quiet. **d** The water (feels) warm. **e** Jack (dived)
off the board. **f** Kristi (loved) her new puppy.
g Anil (has) a blue bike. **h** Lucas (bought) an
ice-cream at the shop. **i** The plane (flew) high in
the sky. **j** The stream (flowed) slowly.

2 a statement **b** exclamation **c** question
d command **e** question **f** statement **g** statement
h question **i** exclamation **j** command

1 a I like netball <u>but</u> Cassie prefers hockey.
b Turn off the oven <u>or</u> the cake will burn.
c The lights dimmed <u>and</u> the concert began.
d I tried to print my story <u>but</u> there was no paper
in the printer.
e The bridge opened <u>and</u> the boat sailed through.
f The waves became much bigger <u>and</u> most of the
people left the water.
g My house is made of wood <u>but</u> Sally's house is
made of brick.
h Be careful <u>or</u> you may spill your drink.

2 a I ate one sausage. I couldn't manage two.
b The wind blew very strongly. Some of the sailing
boats tipped over.
c I like apples. Ben prefers grapes.
d Finish that sheet quickly. There will be no time
for a story.
e We sat on the floor. Mrs Hajika handed out the
notes.
f Alex remembered his boots He forgot his T-shirt.
g I knocked on the door. Mr Hill did not answer.
h The tap must be turned off firmly. It will drip.

1 a We made masks at school. **b** The jellies are set.
c Three friends came to my party. **d** My room
has two windows. **e** My swimming lesson is on
Saturday.

2 a How old are you? **b** Can you tell me where the
pool is? **c** How much do the ice-creams cost?
d What is the name of that animal? **e** Where are
your shoes?

3 a Stop! b Jump! c Duck! d Ouch! e We won!

4 a Open your books. b Do not open your presents.
c Wash your hands. d Bring your work to me.
e Put down your paintbrushes.

5 a Where is Stefan? b Pass the ball to Erica. c That
is a kookaburra. d Who is that? e What a surprise!

Unit 26

1 a canberra, australia b i, tuesday, saturday c the
murray river, australia d my, mrs jackson e pluto
f my, alice g the swan river, perth h fraser island,
queensland i where, mark j i, i k my, the magic
pudding l mayor judi roberts

2 a My favourite fruits are watermelon, grapes,
bananas and pears.
b Don't forget to bring your swimmers, a towel,
a hat and a spare T-shirt.
c I invited Hani, Jo, Max and Andre to my party.
d We cooked the sausages, prawns and kebabs
on the barbecue.
e The four largest planets in our solar system
are Jupiter, Saturn, Neptune and Uranus.
f There were green, red, blue and yellow flags
hanging on the buildings.
g Slowly, carefully and quietly Jani opened
the door.
h Ben ate two kebabs, a steak, two bread rolls
and a bowl of salad.
i My new jumper has red, yellow and black stripes
on the sleeves.
j The scores were seven, four, six, two, eight
and five.

Unit 27

1 a "Are you ready?" asked Mum.
b "That's my red pencil," said Gusta.
c Marc called, "Pass me the ball."
d "There are no more biscuits left," replied Josie.
e "We'll meet this afternoon," agreed Issac.
f "Perhaps you could tidy your room,"
suggested Dad.

2 a "Dinner will ready in five minutes," said Dad.
b Justin replied, "The pencil sharpener is on my
desk."
c "This is a great book," remarked Sam.
d "We went to Melbourne in the holidays," said
Franca.
e "Be careful to hold your ruler steady," advised
Mr Grant.
f Nim said, "I like strawberry ice-cream best."

3 a where, mum b jessica, yes c may I, ben
d i, rachael e dad, this f perhaps, grandma

4 a "There are apples in the fridge," said Mum.
b "Here is my hat," said Joel.
c Ethan declared, "I am nine today."

Unit 28

1 a ? b ! c ?" d , e . f ," g ." h !"

2 a My favourite computer game is Fantasy Forest.
b The largest city in Australia is Sydney.
c "What's the matter?" asked Nadia.

3 a That hat belongs to Jason.
b Have you any library books to return?
c Here is the lid of the box.
d Stop!
e Last year in August I visited the Great Barrier
Reef.
f I have my own dictionary at home.
g "Ouch!" cried Zoe.
h "Turn the television off," said Dad.